The Done List

Ease Anxiety with Small Daily Wins

Angie G. Ford

Sunflower Phoenix Publishing

Published by Sunflower Phoenix Publishing

First Edition, 2026

For permissions, contact: sunflowerphoenixpublishing.com

ISBN: 979-8-9959413-1-6

Printed in the United States of America

The information in this book is intended for general educational and personal growth purposes only. It is not a substitute for professional mental health treatment, therapy, or medical advice. If you are experiencing a mental health crisis, please reach out to a qualified professional or contact a crisis helpline in your area.

National Suicide Prevention Lifeline: 988

Crisis Text Line: Text HOME to 741741

For the ones who are trying.

Even on the days it does not look like it.

This one is for you.

Table of Contents

Chapter 1: The Weight of the List 7

Chapter 2: Why To-Do Lists Can Backfire 17

Chapter 3: The Done List Shift 29

Chapter 4: How to Start Your Done List 40

Chapter 5: Getting Through Hard Days 51

Chapter 6: Building Momentum Over Time 62

Chapter 7: What to Do When You Slip Back 74

Conclusion 85

Resources / Appendix 91

This book is not a substitute for professional mental health care. If anxiety is severe, worsening, or connected to thoughts of self-harm, seek help from a qualified professional or crisis service immediately.

Chapter 1:

When Simple Tasks Start to Feel Heavy

Section 1: What Anxiety Does to Daily Life

You know that feeling before you even get out of bed?

The one where your eyes open, and before your feet touch the floor, the day already feels like too much.

The dishes. The shower. The text you need to answer. The laundry. The email. The phone call. None of it may look huge on its own. But when anxiety is present, even small things can begin to stack on top of each other until an ordinary day feels like an avalanche heading your way.

That feeling is real.

Anxiety does more than make you worry. It changes the size and weight of daily life. Things that should feel simple can suddenly feel heavy, urgent, or strangely impossible to begin. Getting dressed can feel like a project. Making breakfast can feel like one more chance to fall behind. Even choosing where to start can become its own kind of stress.

One helpful way to understand this is to think about your brain like a phone with too many apps running in the background. Even when you are not actively doing anything, the battery is draining. Anxiety works the same way. It uses up energy before you have had the chance to spend it on the day itself.

That is why a simple task can feel so hard. It is not because you are lazy. It is not because you do not care. It is because your mental battery is already being drained before the day really begins.

Picture a morning where all you need to do is shower, answer one message, and tidy the kitchen. On paper, that may not sound like much. But anxiety can turn those three things into mental noise. You stand in the kitchen and think about the message. You open your phone and think about the shower. You head toward the bathroom and remember the dishes. By the time you try to choose one thing, you already feel worn down.

That is what anxiety does to daily life. It makes simple things feel crowded.

The first step is to stop calling this laziness.

Call it what it is: overwhelm.

<u>Takeaway:</u> If simple things feel incredibly hard today, that is not a character flaw. It is a sign that

anxiety is draining energy and making ordinary tasks feel heavier than they are.

Section 2: The Hidden Weight of Unfinished Tasks

There is a kind of tired that comes before you have done anything at all.

It comes from carrying too many unfinished things in your mind.

An unfinished task rarely stays where it belongs. Laundry does not stay in the basket. The email does not stay in your inbox. The phone call does not stay on tomorrow's list. They follow you. They move through the day with you, quietly asking for attention over and over again.

You walk past the laundry and your brain logs it.

You see the unread message and your brain logs it again.

You sit down to rest and remember the bill you still need to pay.

Each task may be small on its own, but together they create a steady mental pull. It is not only the tasks themselves that wear you down. It is the constant awareness of them.

This is one reason anxiety and unfinished tasks feed each other so easily. The more things remain open, the more your mind scans for them. The more your mind scans, the harder it becomes to settle into one thing and finish it. You are not just dealing with the task. You are dealing with the pressure of remembering it, judging it, and trying not to forget the next thing.

Think about a quiet Saturday afternoon. Nothing dramatic is happening. You are sitting on the couch. The room is still. But inside, you feel tense. You are mentally carrying the dishes in the sink, the grocery run, the oil change, the call to your mom, the text you still have not answered. On the outside, you are resting. On the inside, you are hauling around an invisible load.

That is the hidden weight of unfinished tasks.

They take up more space than they should.

And after a while, that mental load becomes its own form of exhaustion.

Takeaway: If you feel exhausted even while sitting still, it may be because your mind is carrying the invisible weight of too many unfinished things.

Section 3: The Shame, Spiral

The tasks themselves are hard enough.

But often the heaviest part is not the task. It is the story you start telling yourself about why it is still not done.

You meant to answer the message. You meant to fold the laundry. You meant to make that call yesterday. Then today comes, and those same small things are still there. That is when shame steps in.

You should be able to do this.

This is not that hard.

What is wrong with you?

That is the shame spiral. It takes a real struggle and turns it into a judgment about who you are.

Anxiety already makes daily life feel harder than it looks from the outside. Shame adds a second layer. Now you are not only trying to do the thing. You are also trying to fight the feeling that something is wrong with you because the thing feels hard in the first place.

And shame rarely helps people start.

More often, it makes them hide, delay, avoid, or shut down.

Think about a phone call you meant to return on Tuesday. By Thursday, you feel guilty. By Saturday, the guilt has turned into shame. Now the problem is no longer the phone call itself. The problem is the feeling attached to it. You do not just avoid the call. You avoid your phone altogether because the shame has made the whole thing heavier than it started.

This is why shame has to be named clearly.

The task may still matter. But the self-attack is not helping.

A more honest sentence is this: This is hard for me right now.

That sentence leaves room for truth without turning the struggle into a flaw in your character.

Shame says you are the problem.

Truth says you are carrying more than most people can see.

Takeaway: Shame is often what makes a hard task feel impossible. The goal is not to shame yourself into action. The goal is to remove the extra weight shame adds.

Section 4: Why Being Understood Matters First

Before we talk about changing systems or building better habits, we need to pause here.

Because if you have been nodding along, if this chapter feels painfully familiar, then you need something before strategy.

You need to feel understood.

So many productivity systems skip this part. They rush straight into solutions. They hand you a planner, an app, a routine, a color-coded method, and tell you to try harder. But if anxiety is already making daily life feel heavy, then "try harder" does not feel helpful. It feels like one more demand.

You may already be trying very hard.

You may be trying hard just to carry the weight of your own day.

That is why being understood matters first.

When people feel unseen, advice can feel like correction. When people feel understood, the exact same advice can feel like support.

Imagine sitting at the edge of your bed in the morning, already feeling late to your own life. In that moment, what helps more?

"You need better discipline."

Or:

"This feels hard right now, and there is a reason for that."

The second response does not magically solve the day. But it removes the loneliness inside the struggle. It makes room for you to stay present instead of immediately turning against yourself.

And that matters.

Because people move more easily when they stop fighting themselves.

So, before this book asks you to try anything new, it wants to start here:

Your struggle makes sense.

The weight you feel is real.

You are not weak because small things feel hard right now.

You do not need harsher pressure.

You need understanding strong enough to make movement possible.

Takeaway: Understanding comes before strategy. You are much more likely to move forward when you stop treating your struggle like a personal failure.

Section 5: A Different Way Forward

What if the problem is not you?

What if the problem is the way you have been taught to measure your days?

Most people are taught to focus on what is left undone. Make the list. Look at the list. Measure the day by how much is still waiting at the end of it. For some minds, that works well enough. For an anxious mind, it can become a steady source of pressure.

It can make the mountain look bigger than your strength.

It can make real effort disappear.

It can leave you doing things all day and still feeling like you did nothing.

A different way forward begins with a different place to look.

Not at the whole mountain.

At the steps you have already taken.

That shift may sound small, but it matters. Because progress grows faster when you can actually see it. And anxious minds often miss progress because they are trained to scan for what is unfinished, missing, late, or wrong.

Think about a morning when you feel scattered before you even begin. You get out of bed. Brush your teeth. Put on clean clothes. Maybe you make coffee. Maybe you answer one message. None of those things seem dramatic. But they are not nothing. They are evidence that movement is already happening.

And when you can see that movement, the next step often feels less impossible.

This book is not asking you to ignore your responsibilities.

It is not asking you to pretend that unfinished things do not matter.

It is asking you to stop overlooking your own effort.

Because the truth is, you are probably doing more than you have been giving yourself credit for.

And once you begin to see that clearly, something begins to change.

Not all at once.

Not perfectly.

But enough to help you breathe.

Enough to help you begin.

Takeaway: The old way of measuring your day may be feeding your anxiety. A better way forward starts by giving your attention to what is real, what is done, and what already counts.

Chapter 2:

Why To-Do Lists Can Backfire

Section 1: The Promise of the To-Do List

There is something deeply satisfying about a blank piece of paper and a pen.

The idea is simple and appealing: write down everything that needs to get done, and suddenly the chaos in your head has somewhere to go. The list feels like control. It feels like order. It feels like relief.

That is why so many people keep making them.

When life starts to feel like too much, the instinct to make a list is not a bad instinct. It is actually a healthy one. You are trying to contain the noise. You are trying to hold your responsibilities in one place instead of carrying them everywhere in your mind. You are trying to create calm.

In that sense, a to-do list is an act of hope.

It says, If I can just see it clearly, maybe I can handle it.

That hope is not wrong. The desire to organize yourself is not wrong. The wish to feel in control of your day is completely reasonable. The problem is not the intention behind the list. The problem is what the list can become once it is written down.

Think about a common morning. Before your feet even hit the floor, your mind is already moving in five directions. Answer a message. Throw in a load of laundry. Eat something. Pay a bill. Remember that phone call. So you make a list. For a moment, it helps. The tasks are no longer floating around. They are in one place. That can feel calming, at least at first.

And that first moment matters, because it explains why the to-do list became such a trusted tool in the first place.

It promises structure.

It promises clarity.

It promises that once everything is written down; you will stop spinning and finally be able to move through the day.

So, if the to-do list has stopped helping you, that does not mean you were foolish to try it. It means you were trying to care for yourself in a way that seemed useful.

That is a good instinct.

The question is not whether you wanted the right thing.

The question is whether this particular tool gives an anxious mind the kind of support it actually needs.

Takeaway: Making a to-do list usually comes from a genuinely good place. It is an attempt to create calm, order, and relief. This chapter is not about blaming you for trying. It is about noticing what happens next.

Section 2: When the List Becomes a Source of Pressure

Picture this.

It is 7:30 in the morning. You sit down with your coffee and your notebook, and you write out the list for the day.

Grocery shopping.

Return that email.

Call the insurance company.

Pick up the prescription.

Clean the bathroom.

Pay the electric bill.

Schedule the dentist appointment.

By the time you finish writing, your coffee is still warm, but the calm you were hoping for has not arrived. Instead, there is a tightening in your chest. Because now it is all right there in front of you.

Every single thing you have not done yet, lined up in a neat column, staring back at you.

For many people, seeing the whole list at once does not create clarity. It creates instant stress. The list that was supposed to organize the chaos becomes the chaos. It stops feeling like a tool and starts feeling like proof that there is too much to do and not enough of you to do it.

When anxiety is already present, a long list does not feel like a plan.

It feels like a verdict.

That shift can happen quietly. You may not even realize it is happening. You only know that you sat down trying to feel more in control, and somehow you stood up feeling more overwhelmed than before.

This is one reason traditional to-do lists can backfire for anxious minds. They gather everything into one visible place, but instead of making the day feel manageable, they make the whole load land on you at once.

A list starts as a guide.

Then, for some people, it becomes a spotlight.

It points your attention at everything unfinished, all at once.

And when that happens, the nervous system often does not respond with motivation. It responds with pressure. Freeze. Avoidance. Shutdown. Not because you are weak, but because your mind is already overloaded.

A good tool should make it easier to begin.

If your list makes you want to shut down, that matters.

It is not proof that you are doing life wrong.

It is information.

Takeaway: A to-do list can unintentionally become a source of pressure rather than relief. If your list makes you feel heavier instead of steadier, that is important information, not a personal failure.

Section 3: The Problem with Measuring the Day by What Is Left

Here is one of the quietest traps in the whole system:

At the end of the day, many people look at their list and count what is left unchecked.

And that number becomes the measure of the day.

You got up.

You got dressed.

You made breakfast.

You answered messages.

You handled something stressful at work.

You drove across town.

You helped someone you care about.

You made dinner.

You kept going, even though you were tired.

But the list does not know any of that.

The list only knows that the bathroom still has not been cleaned. The call still has not been made. The errand still needs doing. So, when you look at it late that night, all your real effort disappears behind the leftover column.

And the day, which was actually full of things you managed to carry, gets filed away in your mind as a day you did not do enough.

This is one of the most painful parts of the traditional to-do list for anxious people. It trains your brain to overlook what was real in favor of what is still missing.

Over time, that becomes its own kind of conditioning.

You start believing that a day only counts if the list is finished.

You start missing the evidence of your own effort.

You start feeling like no day was ever enough, because there is always something left.

And there usually will be.

That is not a moral problem. That is just life.

The problem is not that things remain unfinished. The problem is that unfinished things end up stealing attention from everything you did manage to do.

If the whole day is measured by what remains undone, your effort never gets a fair hearing.

It never gets to count.

And when effort never counts, motivation gets harder to hold onto.

<u>Takeaway:</u> Measuring your day by what is left undone can erase your real effort. The things you did today mattered, even if they never made it onto the list or never got crossed off.

Section 4: Why Anxious Minds Do Not Need More Visible Pressure

Not every brain responds to a list the same way.

For some people, a long visible list is energizing. They see it, feel a spark, and start checking things off. Their brain reads the list as a challenge to rise to.

But for a brain that is already managing anxiety, the same list can land very differently.

Anxiety has a way of turning reminders into emotional weight.

Each unchecked item is no longer just a task. It becomes a small signal that something is wrong. You are behind. You forgot. You are not doing enough. A list that was supposed to help organize the day becomes a running tally of everything that still feels unresolved.

This is not weakness. It is not laziness. It is not a character issue.

It is a nervous system response.

Think about a note on the counter that says call the doctor. It may even feel helpful when you first write it. But then you walk by it in the morning and feel a pinch in your chest. You pass it again at lunch and feel guilty that it still is not done. By evening, the note no longer feels like a reminder. It feels like proof that you are failing at something simple.

The task did not grow.

The pressure around it did.

That is what anxious minds often do with visible reminders. They do not just notice them. They react to them.

So, more visibility does not always create more action.

Sometimes it creates more tension.

And more tension often leads to less movement, not more.

That is why anxious minds do not usually need more visible pressure. They need tools that reduce mental load, not tools that keep unfinished tasks in sight all day long.

This does not mean reminders are bad for everyone.

It means you have to notice how your mind responds.

A tool is only useful if it helps you move.

If it keeps you tense, frozen, or ashamed, it may not be the right tool for this season of your life.

Support should make the next step feel closer, not heavier.

Takeaway: If visible reminders and long lists make your anxiety worse, it does not mean you are doing them wrong. It means your mind may need a gentler tool, one that reduces pressure instead of increasing it.

Section 5: What This Book Is Not Asking You to Do

Before we go any further, let's clear something up.

This book is not asking you to stop caring about your responsibilities.

It is not telling you to ignore the grocery shopping, forget the dentist appointment, or pretend that life does not need to be managed. Your responsibilities still matter. Life still needs to be lived.

This book is also not asking you to become less responsible, less capable, or less serious about your life.

And it is definitely not asking you to become a perfectly organized, highly productive version of yourself.

There is no gold star at the end of this.

No finish line where you finally get everything done and become the kind of person who never falls behind.

That kind of pressure is exactly what we are trying to step away from.

What this book is offering is a gentler way to move through real life. A way to track progress that actually counts what you are doing, instead of only highlighting what you are not. A way to end the day feeling like something counted, even on the hard days. Especially on the hard days.

This is not about pretending every small task is magical.

It is not about forcing gratitude.

It is not about turning hard days into inspirational lessons.

It is about noticing what is real.

Your effort is real.

Your movement is real.

What you did today is real, even if it was smaller than you hoped.

Think about someone who writes a long list every morning and ends the day upset because only two things got crossed off. This book is not telling that person to stop caring about the other tasks. It is showing them another way to see the day. Maybe those two things were making breakfast and finally answering an email they had been avoiding. Maybe those two things mattered more than they have been willing to admit.

The goal is not to excuse inaction.

The goal is to recognize action honestly.

This book is not built on denial.

It is built on a more useful kind of truth.

You still have a life to manage.

You still have things that matter.

You still need ways to move forward.

But you do not need more guilt.

You do not need another system that turns every unfinished thing into proof that you are failing.

What you need is support that helps you keep going.

That is what this book is asking you to try.

Takeaway: This book is not about perfection, denial, or giving up on responsibility. It is about finding a kinder way to see your own effort clearly and move through real life with less shame and more truth.

Chapter 3:

The Done List Shift

Section 1: What a Done List Is

When you already feel behind, the last thing you need is another system that makes you feel worse.

You do not need another list full of things you have not done yet. You do not need another page that stares back at you and reminds you how much is still waiting. What you need is a way to see what is already true.

You are doing more than your anxious mind often lets you notice.

That is where the Done List begins.

A Done List is exactly what it sounds like. Instead of writing down everything you need to do, you write down what you have already done.

That is the whole concept.

You keep a simple record of completed actions. Not the things you planned to do. Not the things you should have done. The things you actually did.

Got out of bed? Write it down.

Made coffee? Write it down.

Took a shower, answered a text, ate lunch, walked to the mailbox, put one dish in the sink, took your medication, folded one shirt, returned one call? All of it counts.

The Done List is not a productivity tracker.

It is not a performance report.

It is a visible record of your real effort.

That matters because anxiety trains your attention in one direction. It tells you to look for what is missing, what is late, what is unfinished, what is wrong. A Done List gently turns your attention another way. It helps you see movement. It gives your mind proof that the day is not empty just because it is not perfect.

Think about a normal afternoon. You may feel like you have done nothing because the kitchen is still messy and there are still three things you have not started. Then you stop and write down what has already happened. You got dressed. You made breakfast. You answered one message. You started a load of laundry. You fed the dog. Suddenly the day may still feel unfinished, but it no longer looks empty.

That is the shift.

The Done List does not deny responsibility. It does not pretend there is nothing left to do. It simply gives equal weight to what is already done.

And for an anxious mind, that can change the tone of the whole day.

Takeaway: A Done List is a simple, visible record of what you have already completed. It shifts your attention away from what is still waiting and toward what is already real.

Section 2: Why This Shift Matters

Where you place your attention matters more than most people realize.

If your mind spends all day tracking what is unfinished, it becomes very hard to feel anything but pressure. Even when you are doing your best, you may still end the day feeling like you failed. Not because nothing got done, but because your attention stayed fixed on what was still missing.

That is why this shift matters.

The Done List is not just a new habit. It is a new direction for your attention. It moves your focus from lack to evidence. From what is still waiting to what is already true.

That may sound small, but for an anxious mind, it changes a great deal.

When you only measure the day by what is left undone, you train yourself to miss progress. You erase effort before it has a chance to encourage you. That makes it harder to keep going, because the day always feels worse than it really is.

The Done List interrupts that pattern.

Think about a day when you planned to do six things and only finished three. If your mind is fixed on the unfinished half, the day feels disappointing. You may go to bed thinking; I did not do enough.

But if you pause and look at what actually happened, the picture changes. You made breakfast. You returned an important call. You took a shower on a day that felt heavy from the start. That is not nothing. That is movement. That is effort. That is a day that contained real follow-through.

Pressure says: You still have more to do.

Evidence says: You are already moving.

That kind of evidence can lower the emotional weight of the day. It can help you feel less buried. It can make the next step easier, because progress tends to create more progress when you are able to see it.

You do not need to deny what is unfinished.

You only need to stop letting it tell the whole story.

Takeaway: The shift from a list of what is undone to a record of what is done changes what your mind has to work with. It replaces some of the pressure of falling behind with honest evidence of forward movement.

Section 3: Why Small Wins Count

One of the most damaging lies anxious people hear, often from inside their own heads, is this:

That does not count.

Getting out of bed does not count.

Eating lunch does not count.

Taking a shower does not count.

Replying to one message does not count.

Those are just normal things. Those are things adults are supposed to do. Those are too small to matter.

That voice is wrong.

On a hard day, getting out of bed is a real accomplishment.

On a day when anxiety has drained your battery before the morning has even begun, making yourself eat something is an act of genuine self-care.

On a day when everything feels heavy, taking a shower, putting on clean clothes, or sending one message you were avoiding is not small in the dismissive way your mind tries to tell you it is. It is real effort.

And real effort counts.

Small wins matter because they are often the first signs of movement. They may not fix the whole day. They may not solve the whole week. But they break the frozen feeling. They remind you that action is still possible.

They are the beginning of momentum.

Think about a hard morning. You wake up already tense. The kitchen feels messy. Your phone feels loud. You feel behind before your feet hit the floor. Then you make your bed, drink a glass of water, and put on clean clothes. Those actions may not look dramatic from the outside. But they are not nothing. They are proof that you are in the day. You are participating in your life. You are not as stuck as you feel.

That kind of proof matters.

If nothing counts until it is big enough, then most days will feel like they did not count at all.

And when nothing counts, it becomes much harder to find the energy to try again tomorrow.

Small wins are not consolation prizes.

They are the actual foundation of change.

Takeaway: Stop dismissing the small things. Getting up, eating, showering, replying, taking medication, tidying one corner, all of these are real wins. Small actions are often the foundation everything else is built on.

Section 4: How the Done List Builds Momentum

Most people think motivation comes first.

They think they need to feel ready, energized, or inspired before they begin.

But for anxious minds, that feeling of readiness often does not arrive on its own.

What creates motivation is movement.

One action leads to another. One completed thing makes the next thing feel less far away. That is how momentum actually works.

And the Done List helps because it makes that momentum visible.

When you write down a completed action, you are giving your brain evidence that movement has already started. You are no longer relying on memory or mood. You can see that something happened. That makes the next small action feel more reachable.

Think about a morning when you feel slow and scattered. You get out of bed, but you still feel behind. Then you make your bed and write it down. A small thing, maybe. But now the day is no longer empty. Then you drink a glass of water and write that down too. Then you answer one text and add that. The day may still feel hard, but it no longer feels frozen. You have proof that you are in motion.

That is how the Done List builds momentum.

Not by forcing you.

By encouraging you with what is already true.

This is also why the Done List can help habits take root. Habits do not form only through willpower.
They form through repetition and recognition. When you repeatedly do something and repeatedly notice that you did it, your brain starts to connect the action with a sense of completion and encouragement. Over time, the action becomes easier because it no longer feels invisible.

It feels known.

It feels counted.

And counted things are easier to repeat.

You do not need to finish everything to build momentum.

You only need to notice that movement has already begun and let that movement count.

Takeaway: Motivation usually follows action, not the other way around. Writing down completed actions helps create visible momentum, and visible momentum makes the next step easier to take.

Section 5: Why Celebration Is Part of the Method

The word celebration can feel uncomfortable here.

You might hear it and think: Why would I celebrate something ordinary?

Why would I celebrate making breakfast, answering one email, or putting on clean clothes?

Because celebration, in this book, does not mean pretending a small thing is a huge achievement.

It means helping your mind and body register that progress happened.

That matters because anxious minds are often very practiced at noticing what went wrong. They are much less practiced at pausing long enough to let something good land.

So, when you write something on your Done List, do not rush past it.

Pause for a second.

Let yourself notice it.

That pause can be quiet. It can be a small smile. A whispered yes. A deep breath. A tiny happy dance in the kitchen. A fist pump by the sink. Whatever feels natural to you.

And yes, a happy dance counts.

Not because you are trying to perform joy.

Because your body is one of the fastest ways to send your nervous system a signal that something went right.

When you move with even a little burst of warmth after a completed action, you are reinforcing the connection between action and encouragement. You are teaching your brain that the day is not only a stream of pressure and demands. It also contains moments of completion, honesty, and relief.

Think about a hard afternoon. You have been putting off one phone call for hours. Your chest tightens every time you think about it. Then you finally make the call. You hang up, write it on your Done List, and do a little happy dance in the kitchen. Not because the whole day is fixed. Not because everything is easy now. But because you did something hard, and you want that truth to stay with you for one moment longer.

That is not silly.

That is support.

Celebration is part of the method because acknowledgment is part of healing.

You are not pretending things are perfect.

You are simply being as honest about what you did as you have always been about what you did not do.

And that honesty changes the tone of the day.

Slowly.

Gently.

Powerfully.

Takeaway: Celebration is not about exaggerating your progress. It is about letting your effort land. A smile, a quiet yes, or a small happy dance can help your brain register that something real went right.

Chapter 4:

How to Start Your Done List

Section 1: Pick a Format That Feels Easy

The first thing to know about starting your Done List is this:

The format does not matter nearly as much as you think it does.

You do not need the perfect notebook. You do not need the best app. You do not need a fresh planner, a color-coded system, or a setup that looks beautiful on social media. If choosing the tool starts to feel stressful, then the tool is already doing too much.

The best format is the one you will actually use.

For some people, that means a small dry erase board on the wall near the kitchen, outside the office, or by the bathroom mirror. A whiteboard works well because it is easy to update in the moment. You walk by, remember what you just did, and write it down.

For other people, it means a notebook on the counter. Or a sticky note near the laptop. Or a note on the phone. All of those count. The Done List is not precious. It does not need the perfect container. It just needs to be visible enough and easy enough that it does not become one more task to manage.

That matters because anxious minds can turn setup into delay. You start thinking about whether you picked the right notebook, the best spot, the cleanest system, and before long you are spending more energy preparing to begin than actually beginning.

So let this part stay simple.

Choose the easiest option available to you right now.

Not the smartest one.

Not the prettiest one.

The easiest one.

Think about an ordinary afternoon. You unload the dishwasher, answer one text, and refill your water bottle. If your Done List is on a whiteboard in the kitchen, you may jot those down in seconds. If it is buried in a planner across the house, you may never bother. The difference matters. A good format supports your actual life. It does not ask you to create extra steps just to notice what you already did.

This is one place where simpler is better.

You are not building a performance system.

You are creating a gentle habit.

Takeaway: Pick a format that feels easy, visible, and natural to reach. The right Done List is the one you will actually use, not the one that looks the most impressive.

Section 2: Start With What Already Happened

You do not need to wait until tomorrow morning to begin.

You do not need a fresh week, a clean slate, or a better mood.

You can start your Done List right now.

In fact, one of the gentlest ways to begin is not by asking: What should I do next?

It is by asking: What have I already done?

That small shift matters.

It takes the pressure off starting from zero. It reminds you that the day is already moving, even if it does not feel that way yet. You do not have to earn your first entry. You only have to notice what is already true.

Maybe you got out of bed.

Maybe you brushed your teeth.

Maybe you fed the dog, made coffee, answered one message, let the laundry run, drove somewhere, or put on clean clothes.

Those things count.

This is one reason the Done List feels so different from a traditional system. A to-do list asks you to stare at what has not happened yet. A Done List invites you to begin with what is already real.

And for an anxious mind, that can be a relief.

Think about a late morning when you already feel off. You did not start the day how you hoped. You feel slow. You feel behind. It would be easy to look at the day and think, I have done nothing. But if you stop and look again, you may realize: you got up, you washed your face, you ate something, you answered one email, you let the dog out. Once you write those things down, the day looks different. It may still feel unfinished, but it no longer looks empty.

That is the point.

You are not trying to create progress out of nowhere.

You are learning to see the progress that is already there.

And once you can see that, the next step often feels less far away.

Takeaway: Start your Done List with what has already happened. You do not need a perfect beginning. You only need to notice what is already true.

Section 3: Count Small Wins on Purpose

This part matters a lot, so read it slowly:

You are going to be tempted to count only the things that feel important.

The bigger tasks.

The more impressive things.

The things that would look reasonable on a normal to-do list.

But if you do that, you will miss the heart of the method.

The Done List works because it teaches you to count the things you usually dismiss.

Getting out of bed counts.

Taking your medication counts.

Drinking water counts.

Making toast counts.

Putting one dish in the sink counts.

Replying to one text counts.

Taking a shower counts.

Tidying one corner of the room counts.

These are not filler items. They are not there to make your list look longer. They are there because they are real actions that took real energy. And on hard days, they are often the most honest proof that you kept going.

That is why you need to count small wins on purpose.

Not only when you feel good.

Not only when the day went well.

On purpose.

Think about a day when your energy is low and your mind feels crowded. You manage to shower, start the dishwasher, and text someone back. Then the old voice shows up and says: That's nothing. You still have so much left to do. This is the moment to count those wins on purpose. Write them down. Let them be seen. Let them stay real.

Because what you count grows in importance.

If you only count what is unfinished, pressure grows.

If you count what is done, encouragement grows.

And encouragement makes it easier to keep going.

This is not about pretending small things are bigger than they are.

It is about giving honest credit for real movement.

Some days, the basics are the work.

Some days, the smallest steps are the bravest ones.

Takeaway: Count the small wins on purpose. The ordinary things you usually ignore are often the truest measure of your effort, especially on hard days.

Section 4: Keep the List Honest and Low Pressure

Because the Done List is helpful, there is a quiet risk that can sneak in.

You may start using it to perform.

You may feel tempted to make the list look fuller than the day really was. You may push yourself to do extra things just so the list seems more impressive. You may start judging yourself if the list is short.

Please watch for that.

The Done List is not a performance.

It is not a scorecard.

It is not a report card you hand in at the end of the day.

It is simply a record of what really happened.

Nothing more.

Nothing less.

That means you do not need to pad it.

You do not need to stretch the truth.

You do not need to write things down just to make the day look better than it felt.

And you do not need to judge the list if it is short.

A short Done List on a hard day can still tell the truth beautifully.

Think about a rough afternoon. You had hoped to do six things, but the day felt heavier than expected. By evening, your Done List says: got dressed, ate lunch, answered one message, took medicine. Part of you may want to dismiss that list because it does not look impressive. Another part may want to add extra things to make it feel better. This is the moment to keep the list honest. Those four things were real. On a hard day, they mattered. Let them stand.

The tool only works if it stays gentle.

The moment it becomes another place to prove yourself, it starts drifting back toward the same pressure you were trying to leave.

So, keep asking one simple question:

What did I actually do today?

Not what should I have done.

Not what would a more productive person have done.

What did I actually do?

That question is enough to keep the Done List honest.

And honesty is what makes it useful.

Takeaway: Keep your Done List truthful and low pressure. A short, honest list on a hard day is more valuable than a longer one built on performance.

Section 5: End the Day by Reviewing What Got Done

At the end of the day, many people replay what they missed.

The call they did not make.

The room they did not clean.

The email they did not send.

The errand they still need to do tomorrow.

That habit can make even a full day feel empty.

This is why the end-of-day review matters.

Before bed, take one quiet minute and look at your Done List.

That is all.

Just read what is there.

You got up.

You ate something.

You handled one thing you had been avoiding.

You got through a hard afternoon.

You made dinner.

You kept going.

That simple review gives your mind a fuller picture of the day. It helps you close the day with evidence instead of accusation. It reminds you that the day may have been unfinished, but it was not empty.

For a lot of people, this becomes one of the most powerful parts of the whole practice.

Because nighttime is often when guilt gets loud.

It is when the mind starts cataloging what slipped through, what did not happen, what will need to wait until tomorrow.

The Done List gives you something real to hold up against that habit.

Not to argue with yourself.

Just to tell the truth.

Think about a night when you are getting ready for bed and already feeling disappointed in yourself. Then you look at your Done List. It says: got dressed, made breakfast, answered one email, picked up the living room, took medicine, drank water. The day may not have gone how you hoped, but it was not empty. You showed up in real ways. Seeing that can change the whole tone of the night.

Keep this review simple.

It does not need to become a journaling exercise.

It does not need to turn into a self-evaluation.

Just read what got done.

Let it land.

Maybe smile.

Maybe exhale.

Maybe give yourself one last quiet yes for making it through the day.

Then let the day close.

Takeaway: End the day by reading your Done List. Even thirty seconds of honest acknowledgment can help you go to bed with more truth and less guilt.

Chapter 5:

Getting Through Hard Days

Section 1: Lower the Bar and Keep It Real

Not every day is the same.

Some days you wake up with a little energy, a little clarity, and a little room to breathe. And some days you wake up and the weight is already there before you have even opened your eyes. On those days, even normal life can feel too heavy to carry.

That difference matters.

One of the hardest things anxious people do to themselves is expect the same version of themselves every day. They wake up on a low-capacity day and still judge themselves by the standard of a better day. They expect full energy from a tired mind. Full output from a strained nervous system. Full follow-through from a day that already feels overloaded before it begins.

That is not fair.

And it is not honest.

On hard days, the Done List asks you to do something simple but powerful: lower the bar to match reality.

Not to give up.

Not to stop caring.

To tell the truth about the day you are actually having.

Lowering the bar is not laziness. It is accuracy. It is reading the situation honestly and adjusting your expectations so they fit the resources you actually have.

A person with the flu does not hold themselves to the same standard they would on a healthy day. A grieving person does not have the same emotional bandwidth as someone who is not carrying loss. And a person in the middle of a heavy anxiety day does not have the same energy, focus, or follow-through as the version of themselves who slept well and woke up calm.

Think about a morning when getting out of bed already takes effort. You look around and see laundry, dishes, emails, and things you meant to do yesterday. Part of you wants to shut down because it all feels too far away. This is the moment to lower the bar and keep it real. Instead of asking: How do I catch up on everything? Ask: What is one kind, honest thing I can do for this day?

Maybe you take your medicine.

Maybe you drink a glass of water.

Maybe you put on clean clothes and write that down.

That may not look like much from the outside.

On a hard day, it is real progress.

Some days are not for big wins.

They are for honest ones.

Takeaway: On hard days, lower the bar to match where you actually are. That is not failure. That is honesty, and honesty is the only place the Done List can work from.

Section 2: Count the Basics Without Shame

On the hardest days, the basics may be the whole list.

And that is completely okay.

Getting out of bed counts.

Taking your medication counts.

Drinking a glass of water counts.

Eating toast on the couch counts.

Brushing your teeth counts.

Getting dressed counts.

Answering one message counts.

Making it from the bed to the couch counts.

These are not things you write down because you ran out of better things to say.

They are not filler.

They are not there to make the list look longer.

They are the truth of the day.

And on a hard day, the truth of the day matters more than any polished version of it.

Shame usually tries to get involved here. It says: You should be doing more than this. It says: These things do not count because they are just basic adult tasks. It says: This is nothing.

But on a day when anxiety is loud and energy is low, these so-called "basic" things are not nothing. They are acts of care. They are signs that you are still showing up for yourself in real, concrete ways.

That matters.

Think about a day when your energy is depleted and everything feels harder than it should. You do not clean the kitchen. You do not catch up on work. You do not answer every message. But you get out of bed. You wash your face. You eat something. You take your medicine. If shame is leading, your brain may file that day away as failure. If truth is leading, the story changes. It becomes a day where you kept yourself going when it was genuinely hard to do so.

That deserves to be counted.

The basics are not beneath the list.

On hard days, the basics are the list.

And they belong there without apology.

Takeaway: Count the basics without shame. On hard days, getting up, eating, showering, taking medication, and doing the smallest acts of care are real wins and deserve to be named.

Section 3: Use the Done List to Interrupt Overwhelm

Sometimes overwhelm looks like panic.

And sometimes it looks like standing in the middle of your own day with no idea where to begin.

You look around and everything feels open at once. The dishes. The laundry. The unread text. The form on the counter. The phone call you still have not made. None of it may be huge on its own, but together it feels like too much. Your mind starts jumping from one thing to the next. The more it jumps, the harder it becomes to do anything at all.

That is where the Done List can help in a very specific way.

On hard days, the Done List is not just a way to track progress.

It is a way to interrupt overwhelm.

It does that by narrowing your focus. Instead of asking you to solve the whole day, it asks one gentler question:

What is one thing I have already done?

Just one.

That question matters because overwhelm often makes the day feel shapeless. It tells you that nothing is moving, nothing is getting done, and everything is out of control. Writing down one finished action gives your brain something solid to hold onto.

You are no longer staring at the whole pile.

You are looking at one completed thing.

That one finished thing becomes a kind of anchor.

Think about an afternoon when the kitchen is messy, your phone feels loud, and you are walking in circles without starting anything. Then you fill a glass of water and drink it. That may seem too small to matter. But if you stop and write down drank water, suddenly the day contains one visible point of progress. Then maybe you wash one plate and add that. Maybe you answer one message and add that too. The overwhelm may not disappear all at once, but it begins to loosen. Your attention has somewhere real to land.

That is the power of interruption.

You do not need to solve the whole day when anxiety rises.

You only need one completed action you can name, see, and count.

From there, the next step often becomes easier to find.

Takeaway: When overwhelm starts to rise, do not try to fix everything at once. Write down one thing you have already done. One visible win can be enough to interrupt the spiral and help you find your footing again.

Section 4: Let Enough Be Enough

There is a particular kind of exhaustion that comes from never letting the day be done.

You do one thing, then tell yourself it was not enough.

You do two more things, and your mind still points to everything left undone.

By the end of the day, you are not only tired from what you did. You are tired from the constant feeling that you should have done more.

That feeling can steal the little bit of relief your effort should have given you.

This is why learning to let enough be enough matters.

It does not mean lowering your care for your life.

It means knowing when to stop turning a hard day into a test you can never pass.

On some days, enough will look different than it does on other days. Enough may mean you got dressed, ate something, answered one message, and made it through the afternoon without shutting down. That may not be everything. It may still be enough for today.

This is a skill.

It does not come naturally to most people who have spent years measuring themselves against an impossible standard. But it can be practiced. And the Done List helps you practice it.

Every time you read your list at the end of the day and let it stand as it is, without adding guilt, bargaining, or but I should have, you are practicing the skill of letting enough be enough.

Think about a low-energy day where you wanted to do laundry, clean the kitchen, return two calls, and catch up on loose ends. Instead, you took a shower, ate lunch, washed a few dishes, and paid one bill. Then night comes, and part of you wants to call the day a failure. This is the moment to pause and tell the truth. The day did not go how you hoped. But it was not empty. You showed up. You carried what you could. That matters.

Enough is not the same as perfect.

Enough is honest.

And on a hard day, honest is far more useful than perfect.

Takeaway: At the end of a hard day, let the real wins be enough. A few honest wins do not mean the day was incomplete. They may be the most truthful measure of the day you had.

Section 5: Build Trust on the Hardest Days

The hardest days are often the days when you trust yourself the least.

You may wake up already expecting the day to go badly. You may assume you will fall behind, shut down, or waste the day before it even begins. When that happens, every small struggle can feel like proof that you cannot handle life well.

That is why the hardest days matter so much.

They are not just days to get through.

They are days that shape the way you see yourself.

On easier days, it is not hard to believe you can function. You have more energy. You can get more done. You feel more like yourself. But trust is not built most deeply on easy days. It is built on the days when things are hard and you still find a way to care for yourself, however imperfectly.

Trust grows through evidence.

Not through pressure.

Not through promises.

Not through shaming yourself into doing better next time.

It grows when you see that even on a hard day, you can still take one honest step.

Then another.

That is what the Done List helps you notice.

It gives you proof that you are still capable of movement, even when the day feels heavy.

Think about a day when anxiety is high from the moment you wake up. You do not have the energy you wanted. Your thoughts feel loud. You do not do most of what you hoped to do. But you get out of bed. You take your medicine. You eat something. You answer one message. You write those things on your Done List. Maybe you even pause for a small smile or a quiet yes after one of them. None of that makes the day easy. But it does tell the truth. You showed up. You stayed with yourself. You kept going in small ways.

That is how trust is built.

You begin to learn that a hard day does not mean you disappear.

It does not mean all progress is gone.

It does not mean you have failed.

It means the day is hard, and you are still finding your way through it.

Over time, that changes your relationship with yourself. You stop seeing hard days as proof that you cannot cope. You start seeing them as places where your steadiness is quietly growing.

The hardest days are not the days the Done List fails you.

They are the days it proves itself.

<u>Takeaway:</u> The hard days are where the Done List does some of its most important work. Writing down even the smallest real wins on those days helps build honest, lasting trust in yourself.

Chapter 6:

Building Momentum Over Time

Section 1: How Small Wins Become Patterns

At first, small wins can feel almost too small to matter.

You write down got out of bed, made coffee, answered one email, and part of you may wonder whether anything this simple could really change the way you move through life. That question makes sense, especially if you have been feeling overwhelmed for a long time. When progress has felt uneven, it is hard to trust small beginnings.

But this is how change usually starts.

Not with one dramatic breakthrough.

Not with a perfect week.

With one small action repeated enough times that it starts to feel more familiar.

That is how small wins become patterns.

A single action may not seem like much in the moment. But when you do it again tomorrow, and again a few days later, something begins to shift. The action takes up a little less mental space. You spend less energy deciding. Less energy resisting.

Less energy recovering from the stress of starting.

The thing that once felt heavy begins to feel a little more normal.

That is what a pattern looks like.

Think about making the bed in the morning. At first, even that may feel like one more thing. You do it once and feel good, then skip it the next day. That is normal. But over time, if you keep coming back to it, the action starts to settle into the rhythm of the day. One morning you notice you made the bed without a long internal debate. That is the shift. It did not arrive with a big announcement. It quietly became something you do.

The same thing happens with the Done List.

At first, writing things down may feel awkward. You may forget. You may feel strange counting small things. But as you keep noticing your effort and recording it, a new pattern begins to form. You start looking for what is done instead of only what is missing. You start giving yourself credit in real time. You start building the day around visible progress instead of silent pressure.

And that changes more than the list.

It changes your rhythm.

Small wins become patterns when they are noticed, repeated, and allowed to count.

Takeaway: Small actions become patterns through repetition and recognition. What you notice and repeat begins to feel more natural over time.

Section 2: What Progress Looks Like in Real Life

Progress rarely looks the way people expect it to.

Most of us imagine progress as something obvious. More energy. More output. More consistency. A cleaner house. A better routine. A stretch of days where everything finally clicks into place.

But real progress is usually much quieter than that.

It often looks like less dread before starting.

Less resistance around a basic task.

A slightly easier morning.

A quicker recovery after a hard afternoon.

A little less shame at the end of the day.

Those things may not look dramatic from the outside. They are still real.

This is one reason people miss their own progress. They are waiting for a big transformation, so they overlook the small changes already happening. They assume that if life is not suddenly easy, then nothing has changed. But that is not how most healing works. It usually moves in subtle ways first.

Think about someone who used to spend an hour dreading the kitchen. At first, they wash one plate and stop. A week later, they wash a few dishes before the dread gets too loud. A little later, they walk into the kitchen and start tidying without the same long mental battle. The kitchen is not perfect every day. But something has changed. The task carries less fear. Starting takes less effort. That is progress in real life.

Or think about mornings. Maybe you still wake up feeling behind sometimes. But instead of losing the whole morning to that feeling, you now get dressed sooner. You drink water sooner. You can reach for one small action before the spiral gets too loud. That matters.

The Done List helps you notice this kind of progress because it gives you something to look back on. It lets you see patterns your anxious mind may miss in the moment. You begin to realize that certain tasks feel a little easier; certain shutdowns do not last as long, and certain wins appear more often than they used to.

Progress in real life is often quiet.

It looks like less resistance.

A little more follow-through.

A little more honesty.

A little more ease.

And that is enough to matter.

Takeaway: Real progress often shows up in subtle ways first. Pay attention to what feels slightly easier, slightly steadier, or slightly less heavy than it used to.

Section 3: Why Confidence Grows From Evidence

Confidence is not something you can force.

You cannot usually talk yourself into trusting yourself. You cannot simply decide to feel more capable and have it become true. Especially not when anxiety has spent a long time teaching you to doubt your own follow-through.

That is why real confidence grows from evidence.

Not from hype.

Not from self-pressure.

Not from pretending things are easier than they are.

From proof.

Every time you complete one small action, you create evidence.

You answered the email you were avoiding.

You took a shower on a hard morning.

You put one load of laundry in the washer.

You made the phone call.

You ate lunch when your appetite was low.

You wrote it on the Done List.

That is proof.

It may look small from the outside, but it matters because it gives your mind something solid to work with. Instead of relying on vague motivation, you can point to something real and say, I did that.

This is one reason the Done List matters so much. It keeps evidence where you can see it.

On anxious days, your mind may forget what you have done and only remember what is still undone. The Done List pushes back against that. It becomes a visible record of follow-through. Over time, that record becomes a steadier source of confidence.

Think about someone who dreads making phone calls. For weeks, they avoid one simple call and start telling themselves they are just bad at this sort of thing. Then one day they make the call. It is brief. It is awkward. It is still done. They write it down. That one moment becomes evidence. The next call may still feel hard, but now their mind has something new to work with. Not just fear. Proof.

This is how trust in yourself begins to change.

Not because you suddenly become fearless.

Because you start collecting enough evidence that fear is no longer the only story available.

Confidence built on evidence lasts longer because it is honest.

It comes from seeing your own pattern clearly.

You showed up.

You kept going.

You did more than your fear said you would.

That is the kind of confidence that grows slowly, but stays.

Takeaway: Confidence grows from proof, not pressure. Every honest win you record gives you evidence that you can keep going.

Section 4: When the List Becomes Less Necessary

There may come a point when you notice something interesting.

You have not written things down for a day or two, not because you gave up, but because some of what you used to need the list for is starting to happen more naturally.

You got dressed.

You ate breakfast.

You answered the message.

You moved through part of the day without needing to write each step down in order for it to count.

That is a good sign.

It means the tool is doing its work.

The goal of the Done List is not to keep you dependent on it forever. The goal is to help you build a new way of seeing your own effort until that way of seeing begins to live inside you, not only on a page or whiteboard.

That is when the list may start to feel less necessary. This does not mean the wins matter less.

It means you are beginning to recognize them more naturally.

Think about someone who first began the Done List by writing down everything: got out of bed, brushed teeth, drank water, took medicine. That level of detail helped because it trained their mind to notice progress. A few months later, they may not need to record every one of those things every day. Not because those actions stopped counting, but because the pattern of noticing has become stronger. They still know those things matter. The list is no longer the only place where progress becomes visible.

That is growth.

It also means the tool can stay flexible. You may use it every day for a while, then only on harder days. You may return to it during stressful seasons and need it less when life feels steadier. That is healthy. Good tools support you when needed and step back when not needed. They remain available without becoming another obligation.

And if life gets heavy again and you need the list more fully, that is fine too.

Needing it again is not failure.

It is just the tool doing what it was designed to do.

Takeaway: When the Done List starts to feel less necessary, that can be a sign that the shift is taking root. Let the tool stay flexible and come back to it whenever you need the support.

Section 5: How to Keep Momentum Gentle

One of the quieter risks of progress is this:

The moment things start feeling better, you may be tempted to push too hard.

You have a few steadier days. The list is fuller. The mornings are a little easier. And a voice shows up that says: Now really go for it. Add more. Do more. Make the most of this. Do not lose momentum.

That voice may sound productive.

But it is often the same voice that created the original overwhelm.

It just sounds more reasonable this time.

This is why momentum has to stay gentle.

The goal is not to take every better day and squeeze as much out of it as possible. The goal is to build a pace you can actually live with. One that helps you keep going without turning progress into a new form of pressure.

Gentle momentum means leaving room for real life.

It means noticing progress without turning it into a rule.

It means letting small wins stay small and still matter.

It means not assuming that because you did five things today, you should always do five things tomorrow.

Some days will hold more.

Some days will hold less.

Keeping momentum gentle means letting that be true without panic.

Think about a week when the Done List has been helping. You have been noticing your wins, doing a few small tasks, and feeling a little more capable. Then one morning you wake up tired. Your first thought might be, I need to keep this going. I cannot lose progress now. That thought sounds motivating, but it often adds tension. A gentler response sounds different: I want to stay connected to what is helping, but I do not need to force today to match yesterday.

So maybe instead of trying to repeat a full productive day, you write down one win, do one small task, and let that be enough to keep the rhythm alive.

That is still momentum.

Gentle momentum is not weak.

It is sustainable.

It protects you from turning support into strain. It helps you move forward without setting yourself up for a crash. And it makes it much easier to come back after hard days, because you are not trying to maintain an impossible standard.

The kind of momentum that lasts is usually the kind that feels kind enough to return to tomorrow.

Takeaway: Protect your progress from turning into pressure. The goal is not intense momentum. It is steady, gentle movement you can return to again and again.

Chapter 7: What to Do When You Slip Back

Section 1: Expect Setbacks Without Panic

At some point, there will be a stretch of days where things feel harder again.

The list does not get written.

The mornings feel heavy.

The old patterns show up.

The house gets messier than you wanted.

The messages pile up.

And the progress you were starting to trust feels farther away than it did last week.

This is not a sign that the method failed.

It is not a sign that you failed.

It is just what real life looks like.

Progress is not a straight line. It never has been. It moves forward, then sideways, then backward a little, then forward again in a way you did not expect. Hard weeks happen. Stress changes. Anxiety flares. Sleep falls apart. Life gets noisy. None of that means you are back at the beginning.

That is why it helps to expect setbacks before they happen.

Not in a pessimistic way.

In a realistic way.

When you expect them, you are less likely to panic when they come. Instead of treating one rough patch like a collapse, you can see it for what it is: a hard moment, not the end of the story.

Think about someone who has been doing well for a few weeks. They have been noticing small wins, writing them down, and feeling steadier. Then a stressful week hits. Sleep gets worse. The kitchen gets messy again. The Done List sits untouched for days. It would be easy in that moment to think, I lost it. But that is not really what happened. The rhythm got interrupted. That is different from losing everything.

Panic adds weight to a moment that is already hard.

It tells you one setback means all progress is gone.

It makes it harder to return because now you are not only dealing with the hard week. You are also dealing with fear, urgency, and shame.

A steadier response sounds different:

This is a setback.

It is not the whole story.

I can begin again from here.

That kind of response leaves room for return.

And return is what matters most.

Takeaway: Setbacks are a normal part of any real process. Expecting them helps you meet them with steadiness instead of panic.

Section 2: Start Again with One Small Action

After a setback, the return can feel bigger than it really is.

You may look at the missed days, the messy room, the untouched whiteboard, the unfinished tasks, and feel the weight of all of it at once. Part of you may want to wait until you feel stronger, clearer, or more ready. Part of you may think you need to fix everything to prove you are back on track.

You do not.

When you slip back, the way forward is rarely a dramatic reset.

It is usually one small action.

That matters because your mind will often make the return feel huge. It will tell you that getting back on track means catching up on everything, clearing all the backlog, or becoming your best self again by the end of the day.

That kind of pressure usually makes it harder to begin.

One small action breaks that pattern.

It gives you a place to re-enter your life without needing to solve all of it at once. It keeps the restart honest. It reminds you that beginning again does not need to look impressive. It only needs to be real.

Think about a day when you have not used your Done List for over a week. The laundry is piled up. Your thoughts feel crowded. It would be easy to think, I need to get everything together today. But instead, you wash one mug. Then you write it down: washed one mug. That one action does not fix the whole week. But it changes something important. You are no longer stuck in the idea of starting. You have started.

That is the power of one small action.

It creates proof.

It lowers resistance.

It gives the next step somewhere to come from.

Getting dressed can be that action.

Drinking a glass of water can be that action.

Writing down one win can be that action.

Answering one message can be that action.

The goal is not to make the restart impressive.

The goal is to make it possible.

Takeaway: When you slip back, do not wait for a perfect comeback. Start again with one small, honest action and let that be your way back in.

Section 3: Refuse the All-or-Nothing Trap

One rough day is not a lost week.

One lost week is not a lost month.

A pause in the practice is not the same as undoing your progress.

These things are worth saying clearly, because the all-or-nothing voice is loud, especially after a setback.

That voice says:

I missed a few days, so I ruined it.

I was doing so well and now I am back to square one.

What is the point of starting again if I always end up here?

Those thoughts can feel logical when you are in the middle of a hard stretch, but they are not accurate. They are anxiety talking. And anxiety has a habit of making temporary things feel permanent.

A pause is a pause.

It is not a verdict.

The growth you built during steadier weeks does not disappear because you had a hard patch. The easier mornings, the reduced friction, the small trust you started to build, those things do not evaporate. They may feel less accessible right now, but they are still there.

This is why all-or-nothing thinking is so damaging. It turns a temporary interruption into a bigger story than it needs to be. It makes restarting feel heavier than it is. It takes one hard stretch and treats it like the end.

Think about someone who used the Done List consistently for two weeks and then stopped for four days because life got hard. The all-or-nothing voice says: Well, I blew it. But a truer response is, I had four hard days. Today I can write down one thing and begin again.

That response leaves room for movement.

That is all you need.

You do not have to get all the way back.

You do not have to fix the whole pattern today.

You only have to refuse the lie that one break erased everything.

Takeaway: Do not let all-or-nothing thinking turn a pause into failure. One hard stretch does not erase your progress. Returning matters more than judging the gap.

Section 4: Use the Done List as Support, Not Proof of Worth This

part matters deeply.

The Done List is a tool.

It is not a scorecard.

It is not a report card.

It is not a measure of your value as a person.

Your worth is not determined by how many items are on the list. It is not determined by how consistently you use the method. It is not determined by how quickly you bounce back after a hard stretch.

You were worthy before the list.

You are worthy on the days when the list is full.

You are worthy on the days when the list has only two items.

This is important because anxious minds often turn output into identity. A short list can start to feel like a judgment. A slow day can start to feel like proof that something is wrong with you. And once that happens, the Done List stops helping. It becomes one more place where shame shows up.

That is not what this method is for.

The Done List exists to support you. To give your effort somewhere visible to live. To offer your brain something real to look at when anxiety is telling you that nothing is working. The moment it becomes a way to rank yourself, it has drifted from its purpose.

Think about a day when your Done List says: got dressed, took medicine, answered one text, ate dinner. Part of you may want to look at that and think: That's all? But the list is not asking whether the day looks impressive. It is simply telling the truth. Those were the steps you took. They matter because they were real, not because they make you more worthy.

The list is there to help you see your effort clearly.

Not to decide whether you are enough.

You are already enough.

The tool's job is smaller and kinder than that.

Takeaway: Keep your self-worth separate from your output. The Done List is there to support you and show you what is real, not to judge your value.

Section 5: Come Back with Honesty and Grace

When people slip back, they often try to come back harsh.

They lecture themselves.

Push harder.

Promise to do better.

Try to make up for lost time.

But harshness usually makes the return heavier than it needs to be.

What works better is honesty and grace.

Honesty means telling the truth about where you are, not where you wish you were.

Grace means meeting that truth without punishment.

Together, they make it easier to begin again in a way that is real and sustainable.

Honesty might sound like this:

I have had a hard week.

I stopped paying attention to what got done.

I feel overwhelmed again.

Grace might sound like this:

That does not mean I failed.

It means I need a gentler way back in.

That combination changes the tone of the restart.

Think about a morning when you notice things have been slipping for a while. The dishes are piled up. You have ignored a few messages. You have not written anything on your Done List in days. Part of you wants to fix everything before noon. Another part of you wants to avoid all of it. Honesty says, I am not where I hoped I would be. Grace says, I can still start from here. So, you wash one dish, write it down, and let that one step be enough to begin.

That matters.

Coming back with honesty keeps you grounded in reality.

Coming back with grace keeps reality from crushing you.

You need both.

Honesty without grace can turn into self-attack.

Grace without honesty can turn into avoidance.

But together, they give you a steady way forward.

You do not need to come back perfectly.

You do not need to come back strong.

You only need to come back truthfully and kindly enough to take the next step.

That is real progress too.

Takeaway: When you need to begin again, come back with honesty and grace. Name where you are, choose one small step, and return without punishing yourself.

Conclusion

Section 1: What You Know Now

By now, you may still have hard days.

You may still wake up feeling behind sometimes. You may still look at the dishes, the laundry, the unanswered message, or the day that did not go how you hoped and feel that familiar weight rise in your chest.

That does not mean you have learned nothing.

It means you are living a real life.

What you know now is simple, but it matters.

You know that overwhelm is real. It is not laziness. It is not weakness. It is not a character flaw. It is what happens when an anxious mind is carrying more than most people can see.

You know that small wins count. Not as consolation prizes. Not as a way of pretending things are better than they are. But as honest, real evidence of effort. Getting out of bed on a hard morning counts. Eating something when you did not want to counts. Taking your medicine, answering one message, making it through the afternoon, doing the quiet, ordinary things that keep a life running when everything feels heavy - all of it counts.

And you know the core shift this book has been building toward:

Measuring your day by what is left undone was always going to make you feel like you were failing.

The Done List offers a different measure.

One that starts with what is true.

What is real.

What you actually did.

And let's that become the record of the day.

That shift does not make life perfect.

But it does make life fairer.

It gives your effort somewhere to live.

It gives your mind something more honest to see.

And sometimes, honesty is the very thing that makes the next step possible.

<u>Takeaway:</u> You know now that the weight was real, your effort has always counted, and there is a gentler, more truthful way to measure your days.

Section 2: What Changes from Here

The outside of your life may not change all at once.

You may still have messy days. You may still have anxious mornings. You may still forget, fall behind, or need to start again. This book does not promise a perfect life. It offers something more useful than that.

It offers a different way to move through the life you already have.

What changes from here is not that every task suddenly becomes easy.

What changes is the way you meet the task.

Instead of measuring the day only by what is unfinished, you begin to notice what is already true.

Instead of letting anxiety tell the whole story, you start looking for evidence.

Instead of rushing past your own effort, you begin to count it.

That kind of change is quiet.

But quiet does not mean small.

It might show up as a morning with slightly less dread.

A day that ends without the usual wave of guilt.

A moment where you finish something small and actually let it count.

A week where you notice yourself following through a little more often, not because you forced yourself, but because the habit of noticing has started to take root.

Over time, those quiet changes add up.

The way you speak to yourself begins to shift.

The way you carry an unfinished day begins to soften.

The way you trust yourself begins to change.

Not because life got simpler.

Because your relationship with your own effort got more honest.

That is what changes from here.

Not everything.

Not all at once.

But something real.

Something steady.

Something you can build on.

Takeaway: The change from this practice is often quiet, but real. It grows in ordinary days, through repeated honesty, and it can change the way you relate to yourself and your effort.

Section 3: Begin With One Win

You do not need to leave this book with a perfect plan.

You do not need a burst of motivation.

You do not need to feel fully ready.

If you have been overwhelmed for a long time, even the idea of starting something new can feel like one more thing to carry.

That is why the way forward begins small.

Begin with one win.

Not ten.

Not a full reset.

Not a promise that you will do this perfectly from now on.

Just one win you can see, name, and count.

This matters because anxiety often tries to make progress feel bigger than it needs to be. It tells you that if you cannot do enough, there is no point in doing anything. The Done List offers a gentler answer:

One thing still counts.

One step still matters.

One small action can be enough to begin changing the tone of the day.

So, start there.

Start where you are.

Start with what is honest.

Start with what you can do today.

Maybe your first win is that you got out of bed.

Maybe it is that you drank a glass of water.

Maybe it is that you made it this far into this book on a day when reading felt hard.

Write it down.

Let it count.

That is your first entry.

That is the beginning.

You are not fixing yourself.

You are not proving yourself.

You are not starting a performance.

You are simply choosing to notice what you did, to write it down, and to let it matter.

That is the whole practice.

And that is enough to begin.

Takeaway: Start with one honest win. Let it be small, let it be real, and let it be enough.

Resources / Appendix

Section 1: Sample Done Lists

Sometimes it helps to see what this looks like in real life.

Not a polished version.

Not a perfect version.

Just a real version.

One of the hardest parts of starting a Done List is trusting that your wins are allowed to be small. Most people who live with anxiety are used to measuring the day by what is left undone, not by what actually happened. So, before you build your own rhythm with this practice, it can help to see a few honest examples.

These are not meant to become rules.

They are here to show you the range of what can count.

Sample Done List: A Regular Day

- Got out of bed
- Made coffee
- Took a shower
- Ate breakfast
- Replied to two emails

- Started a load of laundry
- Took the dog outside
- Put dishes in the sink
- Made dinner
- Folded one basket of clothes
- Read for twenty minutes before bed

Sample Done List: A More Productive Day

- Got up before the alarm
- Made breakfast and packed lunch
- Drove to work
- Finished the report I had been avoiding
- Replied to outstanding emails
- Picked up my prescription
- Stopped at the grocery store
- Made dinner instead of ordering out
- Called my mom back
- Tidied the kitchen before bed

Sample Done List: A Hard Day

- Got out of bed
- Brushed my teeth
- Took my medication
- Drank water
- Ate toast
- Moved from the bed to the couch

- Answered one text
- Watched something comforting
- Made it to the end of the day

That last list is not a lesser list. It is an honest record of a hard day. And an honest record of a hard day matters just as much as a fuller list on an easier one. The point of these examples is not to show you what a "good" Done List looks like. It is to remind you that a Done List is simply a truthful one.

Takeaway: A Done List does not need to look impressive. It only needs to tell the truth about what really happened.

Section 2: A 7-Day Starter Practice

You do not need to turn this into a challenge.

You do not need to do it perfectly.

You do not need to promise yourself that you will never miss a day.

This is simply a gentle way to get familiar with the Done List over the course of one week.

The goal is not to perform.

The goal is to notice.

Day 1: Just Begin

Write down three things you already did today. They can be very small. Getting up, eating, making it this far into the day. Three true things is enough.

Day 2: Notice the Basics

Pay attention to ordinary actions today. Brushing your teeth. Making coffee. Locking the door.

Feeding the dog. Write down at least two basic things you would normally overlook.

Day 3: Add One More

Whatever you noticed yesterday, try to notice one more thing today. Not because the list needs to be longer. Just to practice seeing a little more clearly.

Day 4: Write in the Moment

Instead of waiting until the end of the day, try writing one thing down right after it happens. Finished lunch? Write it down. Sent the message? Write it down. Let yourself notice a win while it is still fresh.

Day 5: Count Something You Would Normally Dismiss

Write down one thing today that your mind would usually call "too small to matter." Then let it matter anyway.

Day 6: End the Day with the List

Before bed, read through what you wrote. That is all. Just read it. Let the list show you what really happened today.

Day 7: Reflect Without Judgment

Look back over the week and ask yourself: What felt different when I paid attention to what I did instead of only what I did not?

This is not about building a streak.

It is about building familiarity.

By the end of the week, you may not feel dramatically different. But you may notice that your effort feels a little more visible, a little more real, and a little less easy to dismiss.

That is enough.

Takeaway: Let the first week be light. The goal is not perfection. The goal is simply to begin noticing what counts.

Section 3: Small Win Ideas

Sometimes it helps to see examples.

Not because you need permission.

Because anxiety can make it hard to recognize your own effort when you are in the middle of the day.

A small win is any real action that helped you care for yourself, move through your responsibilities, or stay connected to your life.

Here are some ideas to help widen the picture of what counts.

At Home

- Made the bed, or straightened the blankets
- Washed one dish, or all of them
- Took out the trash
- Wiped down the counter
- Put something away
- Started the laundry
- Moved the laundry
- Folded a few clothes
- Opened a window
- Paid one bill
- Opened the mail
- Lit a candle or made the space feel better

Health and Care

- Got out of bed
- Took medication
- Drank water
- Ate something
- Ate a real meal

- Took a shower
- Washed your face
- Brushed your teeth
- Put on clean clothes
- Went outside for a few minutes
- Moved your body
- Went to bed a little earlier
- Made a doctor or therapy appointment
- Kept an appointment you were dreading

Work and Responsibilities

- Replied to one email
- Answered one text
- Made one phone call
- Completed one task
- Showed up to work
- Stayed focused for one stretch of time
- Finished something you had been avoiding
- Asked for help
- Said no to something that was too much
- Put one paper where it belonged
- Reviewed one document
- Paid attention in one meeting

Rest and Recovery

- Sat down and actually rested
- Took a few deep breaths

- Put your phone down for ten minutes
- Watched something comforting
- Read a few pages
- Went outside for fresh air
- Took a break before you were completely depleted
- Chose not to push through when you needed rest
- Let the day be enough

This list is not here to make the Done List feel bigger than it is. It is here to remind you that your life contains more real effort than anxiety often lets you see.

Takeaway: A small win is still a real win. If it took energy, care, attention, or effort, it counts.

Section 4: Gentle Reflection Prompts

You do not need to journal every night.

You do not need deep self-analysis.

But sometimes a few quiet questions can help you notice your own progress more clearly.

These prompts are meant to be light, simple, and nonjudgmental. You can use one at a time, or ignore them completely on days when reflection feels like too much.

<u>End-of-Day Prompts</u>

- What did I do today that I almost forgot to count?
- What felt heavier than it looked from the outside?
- What small thing am I glad I did?
- What helped me keep moving today?
- What am I proud of, even if it seems small?

<u>Hard-Day Prompts</u>

- What did I do today that helped me get through?
- What counted today, even if it was basic?
- Where did I show up for myself, even a little?
- What would it look like to let today be enough?

<u>Momentum Prompts</u>

- What has started to feel a little easier lately?
- What win have I been more willing to count?
- What pattern am I beginning to notice?
- Where do I see evidence that I am still moving forward?

These questions are not meant to become another system to manage. They are simply there if you need help noticing what is already true. And sometimes, what is already true is more encouraging than anything else.

Takeaway: Reflection does not need to be heavy or complicated. A gentle question can be enough to help you see what actually mattered in the day.

Also by Angie G. Ford

The Done List for Loved Ones How to Support Someone with Anxiety Without Losing Yourself

You have been working on your own relationship with anxiety. But what about the people who love you?

The Done List for Loved Ones is the companion guide for the partners, parents, and friends who are trying to help someone they love navigate anxiety. It explains what anxiety actually looks like from the outside, why well-meaning support often backfires, and exactly what to say (and not say) during a panic spiral, a freeze, or a hard day.

If someone in your life is reading this book, they may need this one.

Available on Amazon.

About the Author

Angie G. Ford writes practical, compassionate books for people navigating the messy realities of life. Her work focuses on gentle productivity, identity, and finding small wins on hard days. She believes that effort always counts, even when the to-do list says otherwise.

Book Club Discussion Guide

The Done List

1. Before reading this book, how did you typically measure whether a day was productive? Has that changed?

2. What is one small win from this week that you might have previously overlooked?

3. Which chapter resonated most with you, and why?

4. The book suggests that traditional to-do lists can increase anxiety. Do you agree? What has been your experience?

5. What would it feel like to end each day by writing a Done List instead of reviewing what is left undone?

6. Is there someone in your life who might benefit from this approach? How would you share it with them?

7. What is one habit or mindset shift from this book you want to carry forward?

www.ingramcontent.com/pod-product-compliance
Lightning Source LLC
LaVergne TN
LVHW090532110826
845146LV00003B/1067

* 9 7 9 8 9 9 5 9 4 1 3 1 6 *